THE INTERNET SAFETY HANDBOOK

INVESTIGATE!

PROTECT YOUR ONLINE PRIVACY

BY CHARLEY LIGHT

Enslow PUBLISHING

Please visit our website, www.enslow.com. For a free color catalog of all our high-quality books, call toll free 1-800-398-2504 or fax 1-877-980-4454.

Cataloging-in-Publication Data

Names: Light, Charley.
Title: Protect your online privacy / Charley Light.
Description: New York : Enslow Publishing, 2024. | Series: The internet safety handbook | Includes glossary and index.
Identifiers: ISBN 9781978535091 (pbk.) | ISBN 9781978535107 (library bound) | ISBN 9781978535114 (ebook)
Subjects: LCSH: Internet–Safety measures–Juvenile literature. | Computer security–Juvenile literature. | Data protection–Juvenile literature.
Classification: LCC TK5105.875.I57 L54 2024 | DDC 005.8–dc23

Published in 2024 by
Enslow Publishing
2544 Clinton Street
Buffalo, NY 14224

Portions of this work were originally authored by Julie Marzolf and published as *Online Privacy*. All new material in this edition authored by Charley Light.

Designer: Jen Schoembs
Editor: Charley Light

Photo credits: Cover, p. 1 (girls) fizkes/Shutterstock.com; cover (background), p. 1, series art (background) kerly chonglor/Shutterstock.com; p. 5 15Studio/Shutterstock.com; p. 7 Pla2na/Shutterstock.com; p. 9 Andrey_Popov/Shutterstock.com; p. 11 smx12/Shutterstock.com; p. 13 ThomasDeco/Shutterstock.com; p. 15 MPH Photos/Shutterstock.com; p. 17 Monkey Business Images/Shutterstock.com; p. 19 venski/Shutterstock.com; p. 21 Rawpixel.com/Shutterstock.com; p. 23 selinofoto/Shutterstock.com; p. 25 Ground Picture/Shutterstock.com; p. 27 Prostock-studio/Shutterstock.com; p. 29 wavebreakmedia/Shutterstock.com.

Printed in the United States of America

CPSIA compliance information: Batch #CSENS24: For further information contact Enslow Publishing at 1-800-398-2504.

CONTENTS

Words in the glossary appear in **bold** type the first time they are used in the text.

WHAT IS PRIVACY?

Every human being has a right to privacy. Privacy is the ability to keep personal information to yourself. It's also the ability to be alone. This means having space where no one is watching you or listening to you.

Unfortunately, sometimes people don't respect other people's right to privacy online. **Technology** companies and even other internet users may try to get your private information. The good news is that there are steps you can take to protect your online privacy. This book will help you surf the web in peace!

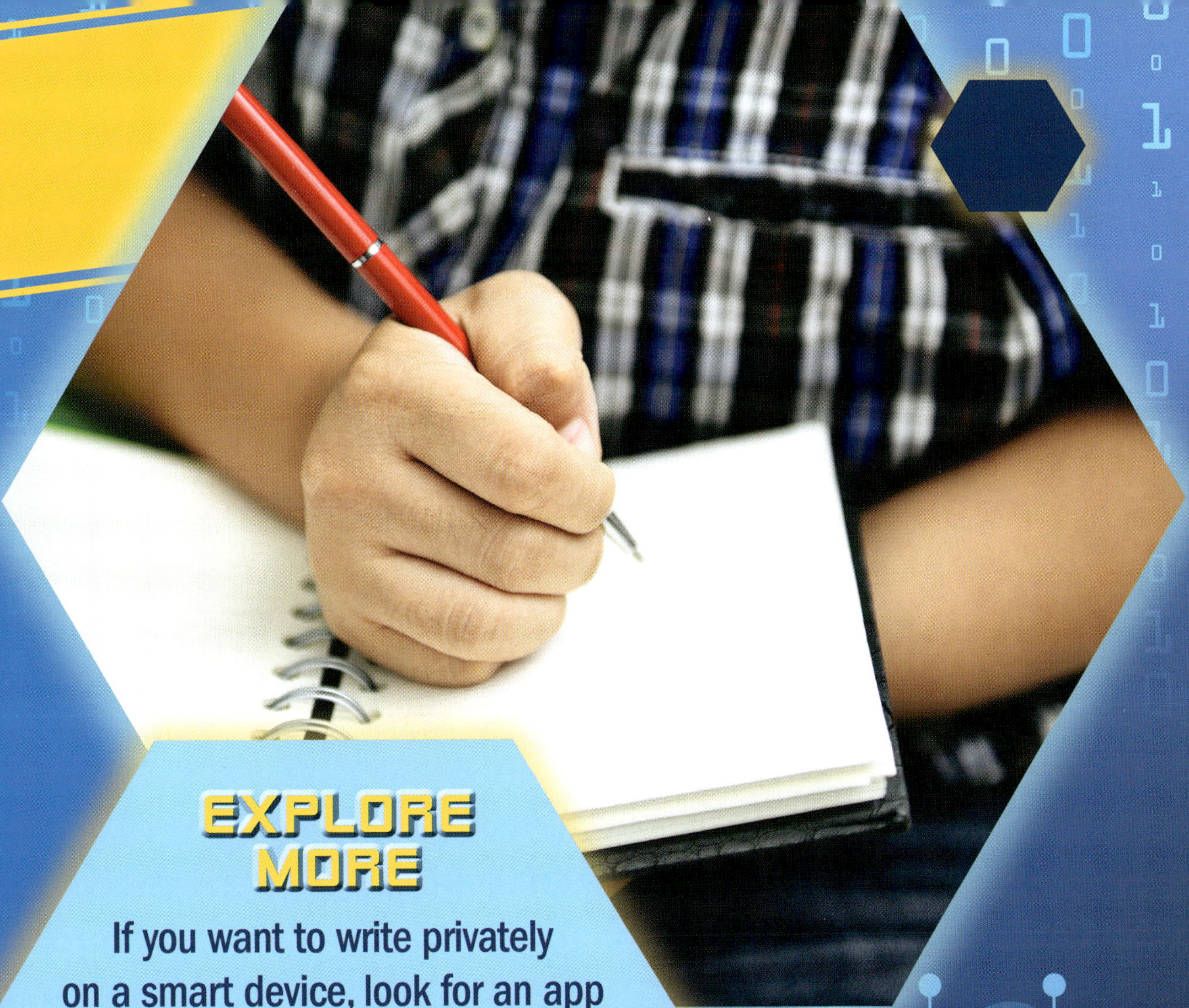

You have a right to privacy, such as a journal no one else reads.

EXPLORE MORE

If you want to write privately on a smart device, look for an app that stores data offline. It will only save your writing to your device—not to the internet. Most journal apps also have locks, so only you can get in.

WHO WANTS TO KNOW?

Tech companies such as Google, TikTok, Instagram, and Facebook collect a lot of private information on internet users. They usually do this to make money. This can be by learning how to keep users using their products. Another way is through advertising. They may also sell users' personal information to data brokers.

Individual people online may try to get personal information about other internet users, too, such as their real names and where they live. Sometimes adults pretend to be younger online to trick and harm kids. These behaviors are **predatory**.

People online may not be who they say they are.

EXPLORE MORE

Data brokers are companies that sell access to information, such as private information about internet users. Acxiom, Epsilon, and Experian are examples of large data broker companies. The laws on data brokers are different from place to place.

USERNAMES AND PASSWORDS

Social media, some gaming sites, and other places you need an account online require you to make a username and password. Your username is the nickname people online will know you by. Your password is a key that unlocks your account.

To protect your privacy online, don't put personal information in your usernames or passwords. Don't use the same username and password across multiple sites. Use a combination of upper- and lowercase letters, numbers, and special characters in passwords. Keep a record of your usernames and passwords written down on paper in a safe place.

EXPLORE MORE

In the United States, the Children's Online Privacy Protection Act of 1998 ("COPPA") was made to keep private information of kids under 13 safe online. It says websites must get permission from parents before collecting information about kids.

Most social media ***networks*** *in the United States require users to be at least 13 to make an account.*

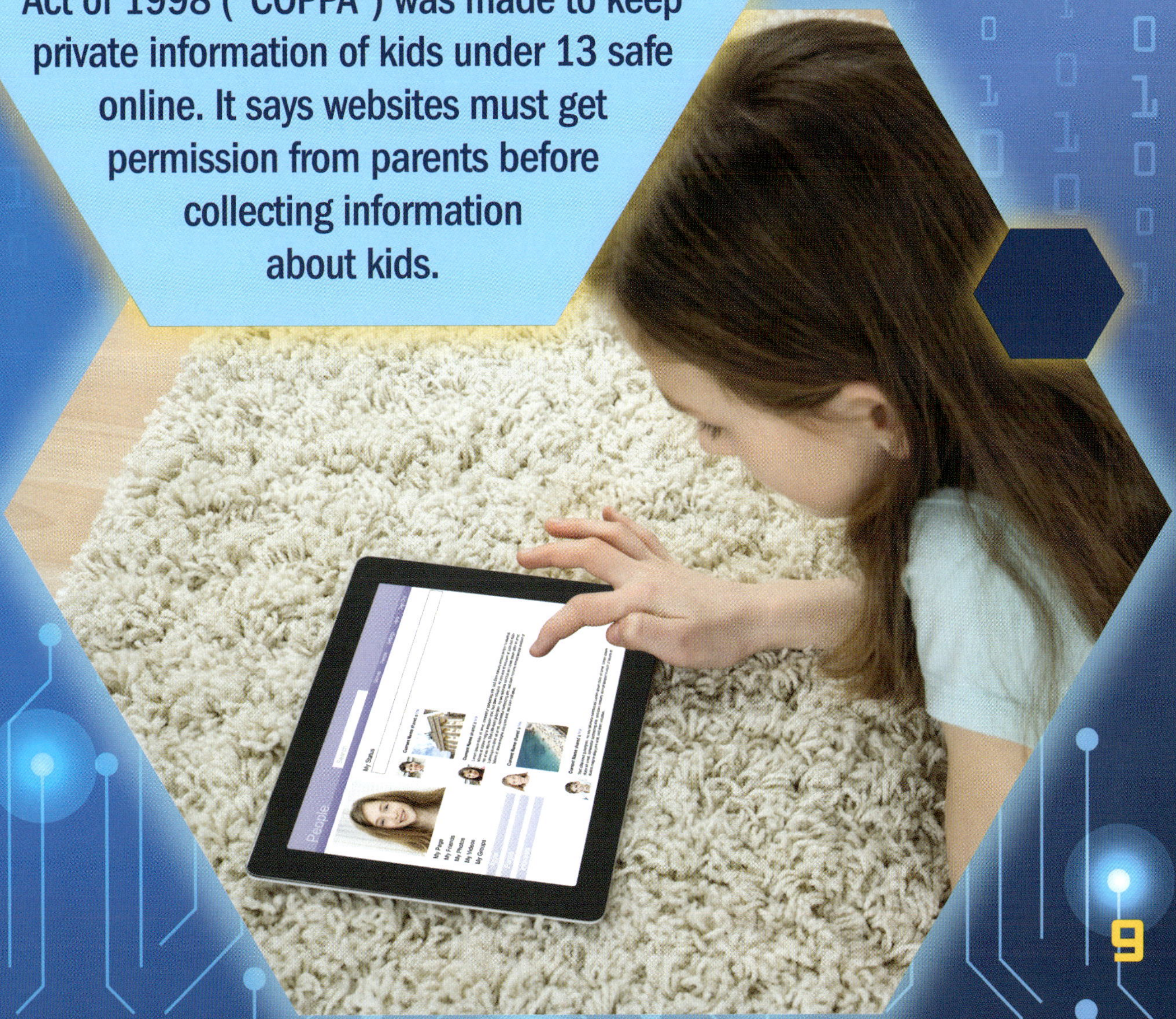

LOCK IT

Just as some diaries have locks on the outside to protect your private writing, smart devices have digital locks to protect your privacy. Many apps have their own locks, too.

Some digital locks can be opened with a personal identification number (PIN). These are often four numbers long. Others need you to type in your username and password. A pattern lock uses a pattern you trace with your finger. Biometric locks use something about your unique **biology**—such as your fingerprint or a scan of your face—to open the lock.

EXPLORE MORE

You can turn on two-factor authentication on some apps. This means you need to log on using two different ways to prove who you are. This protects your information from someone else guessing one of your log-in methods.

Never share your log-in information with anyone other than a guardian.

COMMON DIGITAL LOCKS

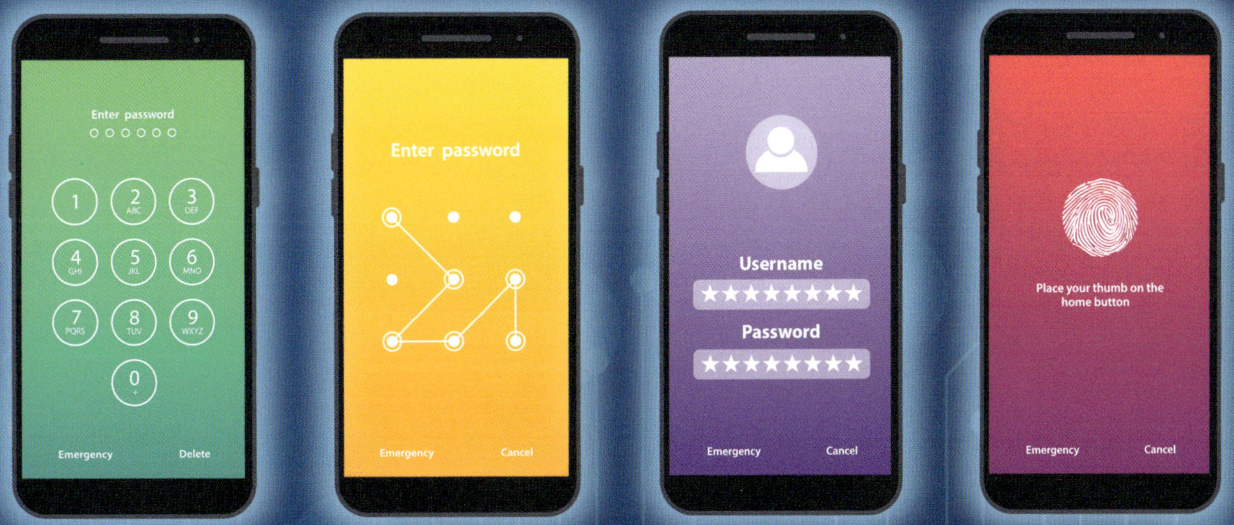

PIN

pattern

username and password

biometric

PRIVATE PROFILES

Most social media networks have an "about me" section on user profiles. You can share a lot about your personality and interests without giving private information, like where you live or go to school. Sharing that you love field hockey is safer than sharing the name of your team or your jersey number.

Social media accounts also have privacy settings. You can set your profile to private, so only friends you choose can see your information. You can even choose which friends can see your posts.

EXPLORE MORE

You can use an avatar on your profile instead of a picture of yourself. Avatars are cartoons or other pictures such as landscapes used to represent you on the internet. They're a fun way to express yourself while keeping your real face private.

On apps such as Snapchat that have a "story" feature, you can also control who sees these daily posts.

PLACES AND FACES

One of the biggest things to keep private online is your location in the real world. This keeps you safe from strangers online finding you in real life.

Some social media offers location sharing. This shows your friends in the app where you are in the real world. You can turn this off under privacy settings.

Never share your location with a stranger online. If someone online asks you questions about your location in real life, such as where you live or go to school, stop the conversation. Tell a trusted adult what happened.

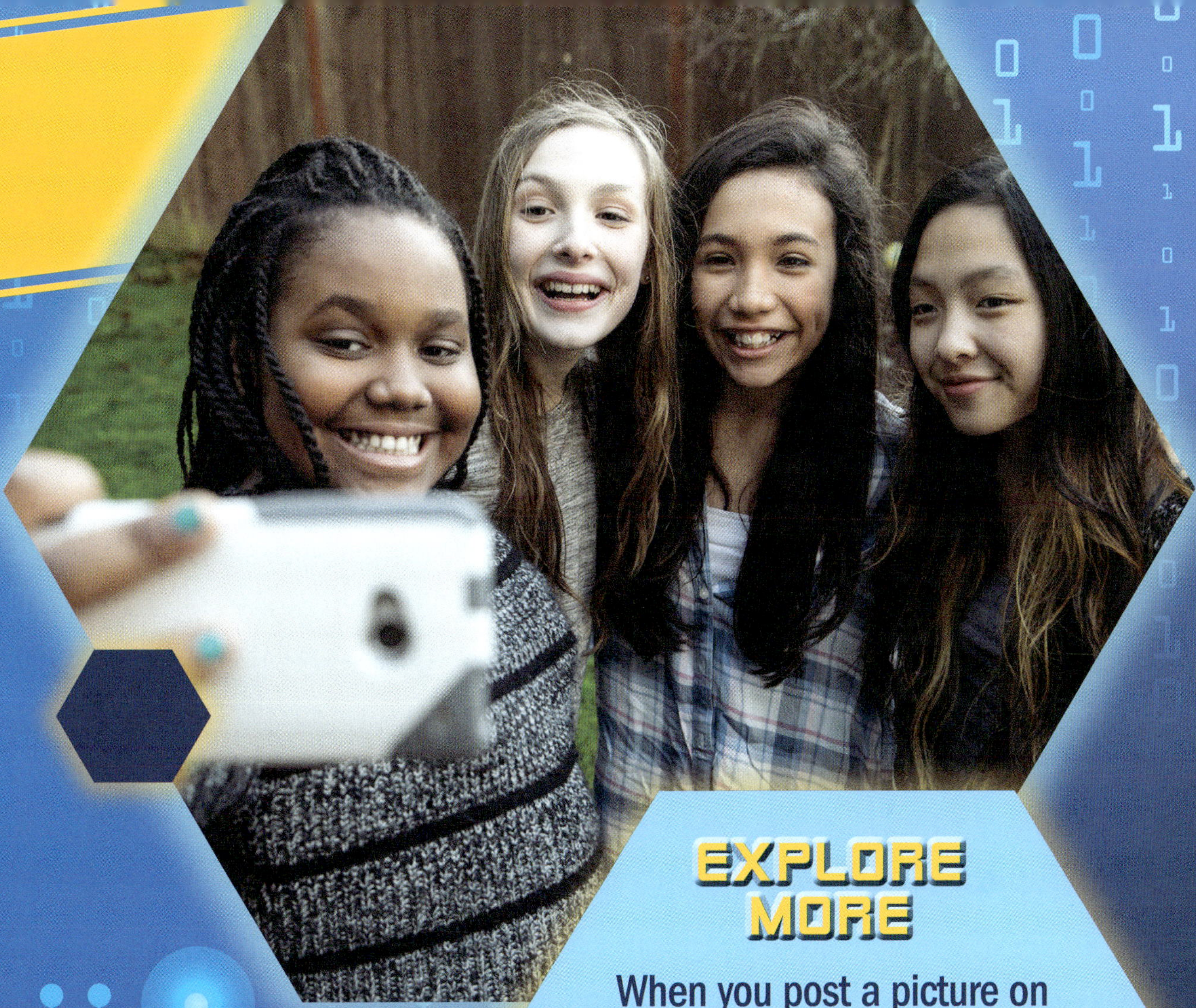

Always ask before you tag a friend, and tell your friends to ask you first, too.

EXPLORE MORE

When you post a picture on social media, you may be asked if you want to tag your location and people in the photo. Other people can tag you too. You can control who can tag you under privacy settings.

PERMANENT UN-PRIVACY

When sharing information about yourself online, be very careful before you hit "send" or "post." Once you do, your information will be there forever. Even if you delete it or hide it, someone could still find it again.

You also never really know what happens to your posts and messages once you share them. Even if your profile is private, your friends who can see your posts could share your information with others you don't know. The same is true for direct messages you send to friends.

EXPLORE MORE

Even if you think you're chatting online with someone you know in real life, it might not really be them. Sometimes people log into others' accounts without their permission. Never give out private information online even if you trust the person. Real friends respect privacy.

If you do share something private online, talk to a trusted adult for help.

JUST BROWSING

You can be followed online by using a **web browser** such as Google. An internet cookie is a text file that stores information about your activity on websites. Some cookies help websites remember things, like the items in your shopping cart. But other cookies can also follow you across multiple sites.

Extensions may also be spying on your private information. Extensions are extra tools you can add to your browser. They do helpful things like block ads on YouTube videos—but many of them also spy on or watch you or hurt your device.

KINDS OF COOKIES

A functional cookie makes websites work, like keeping your items in your shopping cart.

Ad cookies spy on you to send you ads they think you'll like.

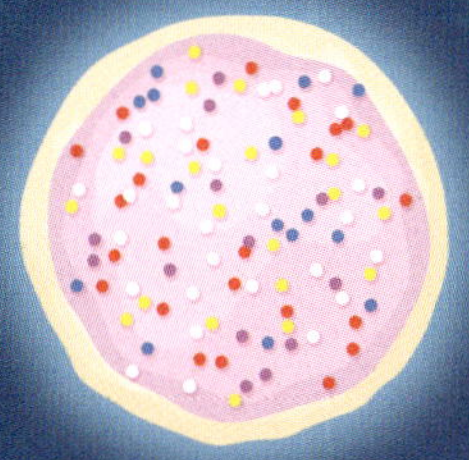

Internet Service Providers use supercookies to spy on your internet use—and you can't block them.

Many cookies are helpful and websites wouldn't work without them. Just watch out for the bad ones!

EXPLORE MORE

A "private" browsing session will delete your search history once you close the browser. Other people using the device won't see what you looked at. However, the sites you visit will still have a record of you.

SOMETHING SMELLS PHISHY...

There are many **scams** on the internet to get users' private information. When a person or group pretends to be a business to trick you into giving them information, they're "phishing." Phishing means using online messages to steal.

Look out for emails and texts that ask for your passwords, account numbers, or usernames. Honest offers, websites, and emails will never ask for those. Don't be fooled by messages saying your account will be closed or that you won't be allowed on a site. This is just a way to try to scare or trick you.

EXPLORE MORE

"Catfishing" is an internet scam that happens in relationships. A person who is catfishing pretends to be someone they're not. They may even use another person's name or photos. They try to get something from the person they form a dishonest relationship with.

Keep an eye out for too-good-to-be-true offers or messages that you've won something. They're often forms of phishing.

SPIES IN DISGUISE

Careful where you click! You might download spyware—**software** that spies on your private information. Companies and people secretly and illegally use spyware to collect personal data, such as credit card numbers, email addresses, and passwords.

Spyware is often downloaded along with something else, such as a free movie or music file. Then it sends your information over the internet to whoever is gathering it. This process can slow down your computer too. Before downloading anything to your computer, ask an adult. It can be hard to get rid of spyware once it's downloaded.

EXPLORE MORE

Sometimes you might come across websites that exist to steal your information. Fake websites often look very similar to the real ones. If you have a feeling an offer on a company's site isn't true, always trust your gut. Check the website's address to be sure.

You may think you're getting something for free, but someone else may be stealing something valuable from you!

STOP, THIEF!

Spyware is one way your identity can be stolen online. Your identity includes your name, your home address, your **social security number (SSN)**, and other private information.

When someone steals your identity, they can pretend to be you. They may open a bank account in your name or spend money using your credit card. This can seriously hurt your future. In 2021, at least 915,000 U.S. children had their identity stolen in some way. The good news is that this is a much smaller number than the year before—1.2 million!

Always get help from an adult when shopping or downloading apps online.

EXPLORE MORE

Lots of scams will try to get you to enter way more personal information than you should. Never enter an SSN or a credit card number online by yourself.

THE "P" IN VPN

"VPN" stands for virtual private network—and the keyword here is *private*! VPNs protect your internet privacy by hiding your location and making it look like you are somewhere else—even another country. This makes it harder for strangers online to find out where you live.

A VPN also encrypts your activities online. Encrypting means turning something into a code that you need a secret key to unlock and understand. This hides what you are doing online from anyone who may be snooping on you. VPNs can't hide your whole identity, though.

EXPLORE MORE

A firewall is a tool that acts like a barrier between your device and the internet. It should let through everything helpful and block anything harmful, such as spyware and other **malware**.

With a VPN, you can see content available in the country you are pretending to be in.

WI-FI WATCH

At last you are ready to surf the web in peace. But one last thing—check your Wi-Fi connection!

There are many public places where you can connect your personal devices to Wi-Fi, such as libraries, airports, schools, and restaurants. But this free service can come at a big risk. Anyone else using the public Wi-Fi can easily see what you are doing on your device. Always use a VPN on your device if you are connected to public Wi-Fi. This keeps your log-in information and other data safe from snoopers!

EXPLORE MORE

If you ever use a shared device such as a computer at a library, clear the browser history and log out of all your accounts when you're done. That way, no one else can easily find your information on the device.

Many libraries teach people how to use technology and stay safe online.

GLOSSARY

biology: The study of living things, including the features that indentify them.

Internet Service Providers: Companies that sell internet access.

malware: Programs meant to harm a digital device.

network: A web of connected things.

predatory: Purposefully hurting someone.

scam: Deceptive acts or operations.

social security number (SSN): A number given to a U.S. citizen that identifies who they are and is used on many legal documents.

software: Programs designed for a computer or device.

technology: Using science, engineering, and other industries to invent useful tools or to solve problems. Also a machine, piece of equipment, or method created by technology.

web browser: A tool for searching pages of the internet.

FOR MORE INFORMATION

BOOKS

Burg, Susan and Renee Tarun. *Cyber Safe: A Dog's Guide to Internet Security.* Portland, OR: BookBaby, 2021.

Pearlman, Catherine. *First Phone: A Child's Guide to Digital Responsibility, Safety, and Etiquette.* London, UK: Penguin Publishing Group, 2022.

Roberts, Dr. Julian. *Our First Talk About Online Safety.* Victoria, BC: Orca Book Publishers, 2019.

WEBSITES

Dinopass
www.dinopass.com
Create kid-friendly passwords here!

HTTP Cookie Facts for Kids
kids.kiddle.co/HTTP_cookie
Learn more about internet cookies—also called HTTP cookies—at this neat site!

Staying Safe Online
kidshelpline.com.au/teens/issues/staying-safe-online
Learn more about how to stay safe online here!

Publisher's note to educators and parents: Our editors have carefully reviewed these websites to ensure that they are suitable for students. Many websites change frequently, however, and we cannot guarantee that a site's future contents will continue to meet our high standards of quality and educational value. Be advised that students should be closely supervised whenever they access the internet.

INDEX